Living with a Gambling Addict

Patricia de León

Published by TR Ediciones, 2024.

LIVING WITH A GAMBLING ADDICT

First edition. March 1, 2024.

ISBN: 979-8224217618

Written by Patricia de León.

Dedicated to all the individuals who suffer due to the addiction of someone close

Introduction

This is a true story, one that I have experienced firsthand as a family member of a gambling addict. I never imagined that gambling addiction would become a part of my life, but I had no choice in the matter. Now that my father is no longer with us, I can share how I lived through his addiction. I can now recount with more emotional distance and without resentment what I felt. And I have decided to do so because I would like my testimony to help others who may be going through something similar.

I have experienced how gambling destroys those who play and their surroundings. It was years filled with mixed emotions: pain, anger, hatred, despair, compassion, sadness, helplessness... I imagine those who are living under these circumstances will feel identified.

Addictions are a harsh test for the addict and their family. It is very painful to witness a loved one self-destruct and at the same time try to understand what drives them to inflict so much harm on themselves and others. For the compulsive gambler, their sole obsession is gambling, and except for rare exceptions, they do not stop to think about the suffering of those around them. I believe this is common to any addiction.

I will not claim in these pages that my father quit gambling because that would be a lie. I am convinced that there are solutions, but they only work if the compulsive gambler is willing to make an effort. It was difficult for me to accept this, but sometimes there is no other choice. I also understood that, despite everything, life goes on and that, although the problem is always there, one can and should be happy.

If I had known certain things about my attitude and way of reacting beforehand, I believe I would not have taken so long to make certain decisions, and I would have saved myself a lot of emotional distress.

When I had to confront this situation, I found that there was little literature dedicated to the family members and other close individuals of the compulsive gambler. I contacted several specialized associations where I found good intentions but little hope because, according to the people I spoke with, it was almost impossible for an elderly person like my father to quit gambling. Unfortunately, they were right. But what do you do when you have an absolute emotional blockage and don't know where to start or what steps to take? How do you know what is best for everyone? How much can and should you help? Where is the limit?

If you are reading this book, I suppose someone close to you has been caught up in gambling. Or perhaps you are the compulsive gambler yourself. I hope that in these pages, you find ideas that inspire and help you. I recount in maximum detail what I lived through, with its ups and downs—more of the latter in my case—and with everything I have learned along the way.

This is how it all began.

People say that when something important happens, you remember in detail what happened at that moment: where you were, what time it was, what you were doing. Well, among those moments that I will never forget is the day I found out that my father was hooked on slot machines. Without a doubt, I can say that there is a before and an after that day.

It was June 11th, around noon. I was at a work lunch when I received a call from my cousin. Since she lived near my parents, and my mother was sick those days, I thought before answering that something had happened to my mother. That's why the first thing I asked was if my mother was okay, and she said yes, but that she wanted to talk to me when she was calm. That made me even more nervous, so I got up from the table for a moment and stepped outside the restaurant.

She explained that the day before, she had bumped into my father at a café. They had coffee together, and when my father left, the café owner, who was a friend of my cousin's, asked her how she knew my father. When she told her that he was her uncle, the lady told her that my father spent a lot of money on slot machines, that he went there every day with several 50 euro bills that he would spend on the game. Apparently, she felt sorry seeing him so hooked that one day she turned off the machine, which made him very angry, according to her, and told him that it was broken. Some acquaintances who saw him frequently at that bar also warned him that he was gambling too much, but obviously, he didn't care. Shamelessly, he would ask for change for his bills over and over again until he got tired or, probably, until he had nothing left.

I couldn't believe what I was hearing. My father was already 78 years old, and many of those years he had been dealing with fragile health.

He was independent but with limitations and walked with considerable difficulty. He constantly complained about how bad he felt and always said he could hardly walk. He made excuses to go to many places, although, as I later discovered, he mustered up the strength to go to the bank to get money and then to bars to spend it. I also found out that he would take buses to go and gamble in other areas of the city where he wasn't known.

All of this seemed impossible to me because for years his health had been delicate. When he was 55, he had a stroke, and since then, he had undergone a series of complex surgeries and illnesses that had left him with significant sequelae. In fact, he couldn't return to work. He had been on the brink of death several times, but he managed to survive because he had great willpower. It's true that his character had changed; he had become much more irritable, but I always attributed this to his illness, and in a way, it seemed understandable given his suffering, although sometimes he would have these outbursts of disproportionate anger, especially towards my mother. Over time, I understood that behind those monumental fits of rage, there were probably other reasons, such as the bitter disappointments of gambling.

To me, he had always been an exemplary father, hardworking, honest, and with a good sense of humor. He emphasized the importance of good behavior so much that he even dared to reproach certain actions of his closest relatives. He always seemed exemplary in everything. However, I had just discovered a side of him that I didn't recognize, nor did my mother or my sisters. In fact, with some naivety, I sometimes thought that my cousin had been misinformed.

However, the reality was that my cousin confessed to us later that she had been observing for quite some time that my father was gambling worryingly on slot machines, but she hadn't dared to tell us until then.

She told us that she had talked to him on one occasion, and he responded angrily that it was his money and he could spend it however he wanted.

This was a very typical reaction from my father, even before he began to have fragile health. He was used to always getting his way and imposing his will. Deep down, we all knew him well, and that's why, from the very beginning, we knew that we were dealing with a very difficult situation, not only because of his addiction itself but also because my father had never accepted advice from anyone.

Despite the idealized image I had of him, my father, like many of his generation, was a sexist man firmly convinced that his authority was above that of my mother, who had spent many years in their marriage yielding to avoid confrontation. It was undeniable that in recent years, he would get angry more often, and everything seemed to bother him, but I always believed that this bitterness was due to his illness, which had imposed many restrictions on him.

At times, I thought it was unfair for him to behave like that towards us, especially towards my mother, who bore the brunt of it. But in the end, my compassion for him and his circumstances always prevailed. In one way or another, I always justified his difficult character because he also had phases of good humor, generosity, and kindness that more than compensated for his flaws. Now I think that these reactions were a way for him to manipulate us.

The First Steps

The reality was that my mother, sisters, and I knew that the situation was particularly complicated. The first thing my cousin and I did was to talk to my mother and sisters to explain the situation to them. Needless to say, they were also astonished.

My mother had never been concerned about money because traditionally it was my father who took care of going to and from the bank. When we learned about his gambling addiction, we asked my mother if she hadn't noticed anything or if she had observed any changes in his behavior. She ended up admitting that she noticed the money he brought home was being spent very quickly, and she would occasionally mention it to him. My father always responded that everything was too expensive and that with how rarely he went out and how sick he was, he could hardly spend anything. So my mother kept quiet, and the conversation ended. The last thing she imagined was that he was spending it on slot machines.

Apart from that, my mother had no idea about what they had in the bank or whether he had spent their savings or not. I believe she acted irresponsibly in this regard because, despite my father's sexism, she should have been interested in his financial situation and not turned a blind eye.

The first thing we did the day after my cousin's call was to go with my mother to the two banks where they had accounts without my father knowing, to find out how things stood. The previous night—and many more would follow—I couldn't sleep, speculating about how much money he could have spent.

Since it seemed so hard to believe, I was inclined to think that it was a recent and passing hobby, but I feared he might have emptied the accounts or even put them in the negative. I had heard that some gamblers lost thousands of euros in no time, and I didn't rule out the possibility that my father was one of them.

And indeed, he was. The accounts were nearly empty, and we were told that there had been significant overdrafts that my father had been covering with a lifetime of savings. The good news was that there were still a couple of fixed-term deposits that he hadn't been able to touch because he needed my mother's consent. Not that he had done it out of consideration for her. Simply, the financial institution had set it up that way by default, and luckily for my mother, in this case. For now, that money was safe for a couple more years.

We also took the opportunity to request online banking access codes so that we could monitor the transactions without his knowledge. My sisters and I were authorized on all the accounts, but we had never considered doing something like that before. Now it seemed necessary because we were facing a very complicated situation, and we couldn't close our eyes to it. We needed to know exactly what we were up against.

My innate curiosity and my natural tendency to want to solve everything led me to embark on a solo investigative work from that moment on, keeping my sisters and mother informed—and they agreed with what I was doing—but they never actively participated. I have always had the role of the older sister that led me to shoulder too many responsibilities, even if no one asked me to. Sometimes I've had the feeling that others categorize you and end up seeing it as something natural.

Now I know that I have a codependent nature, something I will explain later, and thanks to my father's addiction (everything has a positive side), I understood that I needed to learn to live in a healthier way.

From the very beginning, my mother and sisters stayed out of it, without monitoring, I don't know if out of fear of my father's reaction or not wanting to know the reality. I don't criticize them because I think their reaction is just as valid as mine. Everyone is different and faces events in the best way they can. They have always respected my attitude, and I have respected theirs. In fact, on many occasions, considering the great disappointments I experienced, I came to think that I should have responded the same way they did. That way, I would have saved myself a lot of suffering. However, I was unable to not get involved. As I said, I had not yet understood that this was not the best way to help my father, my family, or myself.

The Magnitude of the Events

At times, in an attempt to downplay the situation, I tried to reassure myself by thinking that if there was still some money in the bank and my parents weren't bankrupt, maybe this wasn't such a big deal. However, I decided to find out the real extent of my father's addiction and understand what we were truly facing.

My mind was racing and filled with so much confusion that amidst all the information and overwhelming thoughts, I even started to think that maybe my mother was also spending too much. Although we had been alerted about my father and I was almost certain that the cash he withdrew from the bank was largely for his expenses. I sometimes doubted my mother. It didn't take long to clarify this point, and as expected, there were no more surprises.

First, I reviewed the account transactions from recent years, and then I confirmed that it wasn't just a sporadic hobby. The volume of cash withdrawals was very high, and despite my parents having two pensions and incomes well above average, they would spend more than they earned in many months. Moreover, the spending trend was increasing, especially in recent years. Until three years ago, they had been adding some money—not much—to their savings, but that had stopped, and the process was exactly the opposite. My father had started spending a lifetime of savings on gambling, and only what he couldn't withdraw and the jointly owned property with my mother remained, which he couldn't sell without her consent.

After verifying that it wasn't a recent or passing hobby, the next step was to try to find out how long my father had been gambling. To my great surprise, when I reviewed the savings passbooks kept at home, I saw that my father had been gambling and systematically spending at least half of his income for over 20 years.

Since my parents received two substantial pensions, I realized that for years they had covered their regular expenses with one pension, while the other went entirely to slot machines. There were some variations from month to month, but they were minimal. On the other hand, it was noteworthy that their lifestyle didn't involve great luxuries. My mother has always been rather austere and not prone to indulgence, so her few needs had been more than adequately met.

I also found it striking that until relatively recently, my father had maintained some control over the situation. In other words, he had been spending a lot of cash for decades, but in a sustained manner, without major fluctuations. Perhaps he was an atypical gambler, I don't know, but that apparent control, without conspicuous extremes of spending, had allowed him to skillfully hide his addiction all that time.

Furthermore, like many marriages of their time, my father had always had control over financial matters and took care of going to the bank for money, so he did as he pleased without my mother asking for explanations. Additionally, at family gatherings, he would occasionally boast proudly that they had a good amount of savings, and my sisters and I believed it. It wasn't surprising because, in theory, their situation was much better than that of many other retirees, and since my father's health was delicate, they never went on trips or made significant extraordinary expenses. Quite frequently, my parents had generous gestures towards us, our husbands, and our children.

After discovering everything and reflecting so much on the subject, I realized that in recent years, they hadn't been as generous, but until then, we hadn't noticed anything, among other reasons because we have never placed too much importance on money. If they gave us something, it was perfect. If not, it was also fine.

Upon realizing how my father had managed to maintain the same level of spending for so many years, one of the preconceived notions I had about gambling addicts shattered. The news I had heard in the media about gambling addiction had led me to believe that compulsive gamblers easily fell into a cycle of excessive spending that quickly led them to ruin and borrowing money to satisfy their desperate need. This was also confirmed to me by some gambling addicts in the process of rehabilitation whom I spoke with for this book, and, I must admit, to better understand my father.

However, from what I could see, the gambling had been an expensive —hobby— for my father for many years, one he could afford, only to become a monster that he couldn't control and that completely alienated him in the last stage of his life.

It took me just a couple of days to form a fairly accurate picture of the situation. Meanwhile, my mother, my sisters, and I had agreed to meet with him over the weekend to explain what we had been told, without revealing my cousin's involvement, of course. We hadn't warned him about anything; we believed it was better to address the issue together, the four of us, without any preamble. My sisters were out of town, so we decided to wait until the three of us could gather. We thought it was essential for him to see us united in this matter.

The First Face-to-Face Encounter

Only four days passed until we spoke with him, but they felt like an eternity. My sisters and I had been living away from his house for years, but we would often visit with our husbands and children, sometimes staying with them for a few days. I was the one who went most frequently with my two kids. My husband worked out of town on many weekends, which allowed me to take the opportunity to visit my parents, at least one weekend a month.

I think we were all very nervous because we were terrified of the moment when we had to tell him what we knew. We were afraid of his reaction because, as I mentioned before, my father had a difficult temperament. I still remember those days with anguish, my lack of concentration, my irritability at home, the sleepless nights, the constant anxiety.

However, this first confrontation turned out to be easier than we imagined. I believe it was simply because we caught him off guard, and he had little capacity to react. It was me who started talking to him, remaining composed and polite throughout:

—Dad, we are extremely concerned about something we have heard, and we don't know if it's true. We have been told that you spend a lot of money on slot machines.

At that moment, his expression changed drastically, and he became very serious, but he reacted well, without aggression:

—Well, I don't have any problem. I play a little occasionally, but nothing more.

—Can we help you in any way?

—No, because I'm telling you I hardly play. —He was already a bit defensive—. But if I go to the bar to have a coffee and can't talk to anyone. —He had chronic aphonia because of a difficult surgery—. Sometimes I put a coin to entertain myself.

—Dad, we hope it's as you say. We're worried that you might lose control of this, and it could get out of hand. You know that can happen without you even realizing it —we nodded—, and it would be heartbreaking if, after all the hard work you and mom have put in your whole lives, you find yourselves in a terrible financial situation because of something like this.

—Well, I also have the right to have some entertainment... And considering how bad I am and how little time I have left... —He became more defensive and played the victim, something very common for him.

—Dad, we're not judging you. —One of my two sisters said to defuse the tension—. We just want you to tell us if you're in trouble and if this is more than an occasional hobby because, in that case, you would need help. And we're here for whatever you need. We're a family, and we want you to know that you're not alone.

—I know, but it ends today. I hardly play, only sometimes, but it's over now. There's nothing more to talk about. It's done. I won't go to the bars anymore, and the matter is settled.

—Perfect, Dad. It's not about going anywhere. There are bars without slot machines, and you can go to other places for entertainment. We just want you to be well, that's all.

And that's how the conversation ended, more or less. We managed to have a dialogue with him, and I was surprised that he even thanked us for bringing it up, which was unusual for him. We all breathed a sigh of relief at that moment.

I don't know what conclusion my mother, who didn't dare to speak during the conversation, and my sisters drew from it. I, reluctantly and with the information I had gathered, knew he was lying and that this was just the beginning, but I didn't want to appear defeatist in front of them.

I thought my father deserved some trust, and I also wanted to believe that he would keep his promise to quit gambling. He said it with great conviction, but I never fully believed him. Not because he didn't intend to quit, but because I knew it was almost impossible. I was well aware that I had been a heavy smoker for years, and it was incredibly challenging for me to quit. I knew what it was like to be dependent and that, even with a strong willpower, it often fails you. That's why I sensed that my father, even if he wanted to, couldn't quit gambling without subjecting himself to very strict rules regarding money usage. And I wasn't wrong.

Only Good Intentions

I'm sure my father tried to quit gambling for a while after the first conversation we had with him, but as expected, he couldn't do it on his own. I also noticed that a few hours after talking to him, when I called my parents' house at night to let them know I had arrived safely at my destination after a trip I had to take, his tone had changed drastically. He seemed distant, I would even say angry, after reflecting on what we had told him, but I didn't pay much attention to it.

Naively, I thought it was just my assumption because, based on my logical reasoning (which I later realized had nothing to do with his way of understanding things), it didn't make sense for him to be upset now when a while ago he had reacted so sensibly. Besides, we hadn't reproached him in any way, only offered words of support. That was my way of thinking, and once again, I was wrong, as I later found out.

On the other hand, with great distress and disappointment, I realized that my father's promise to quit gambling lasted only three days. That's how long it took for him to go and make the next withdrawal. He took out less money than usual, but within two days, he was back for more. And in a matter of weeks, he was spending more than he had in the previous months.

I knew that at some point, we would have to talk to him again because it was evident that he had a full-blown addiction. I also knew that finding a solution wouldn't be easy because my father wouldn't accept any of the control and deprivation measures recommended by experts.

Without going into details, I asked my mother if she had noticed any change in his behavior. I remember she told me that since the day we all gathered to talk with him, they always went to the bank together to withdraw money, and he asked her to keep it. He also handed over the bank cards, I suppose to avoid the temptation of using the ATM. She seemed content with my father's behavior.

I also believe that, at least for a very specific period, my father wanted to quit playing. However, his addiction overwhelmed him. He never stopped withdrawing money behind my mother's back, and even though he no longer used the ATM because he didn't have the cards, he would still withdraw money separately at the bank counter when he could.

Despite all these gestures that demonstrated his good intentions, ten days after our first conversation, he had already spent a month's salary. It was agonizing for me to think about the vulnerable situation my parents could end up in because of all this. This thought haunted me for years because my parents were already elderly, and I feared that if we didn't find a solution, they would go from having complete financial security to having nothing. It terrified me when I heard from some friends about the expenses, they were incurring for a nursing home or a live-in caretaker for their parents. I kept silent, but I was well aware that my parents could find themselves in that need at any moment, and the cursed gambling could put them in a precarious situation.

All of this made me angry with my father. I felt it was unfair what he was doing because he was also putting my mother in a very compromising position. Yet, we were afraid to confront him.

With this whirlwind of thoughts, I spiraled into an obsessive cycle that caused me immense distress. Every day, I would check my parents' accounts with the fear that my father had left them in negative balance. I still remember the pounding of my heart before checking what my father had done each day. If he hadn't made any withdrawals, I would breathe a sigh of relief until the next day. If he had withdrawn money, the disappointment was twofold, and my anxieties multiplied. It was absurd, looking back now, because it didn't solve anything; it only caused me more pain. However, I couldn't stop myself from being in control.

External Help

One of my next steps was to contact a gambling support association in my father's city. I called them with a fair amount of skepticism because I knew my father would never want to go there in any way, but I needed to hear their opinion.

It was a difficult conversation because they made it clear to me from the beginning. The person who attended to me bluntly told me that my father would never recover at his age.

—How old is your father? —He asked me.

—Seventy-eight —I replied.

—Buff... Forget it. Your father is not going to stop gambling.

This hit me like a cold shower, and I reacted with some anger towards the person I was speaking to. Perhaps because I hadn't fully come to terms with having a gambling addict for a father. The last thing I needed was for someone, right at the beginning of the conversation, someone accustomed to dealing with this illness, to tell me that there was nothing to be done except to resign ourselves. Was this how they helped people? I thought I would be talking to someone more diplomatic, at least someone with a bit more tact and empathy. I felt so contradicted that I responded without hiding my anger.

—Look, there must be some solution. —I replied, not hiding my disagreement—. I'm not saying it's easy, but why are you so sure that my father won't change?

—Because your father is already very old, and at that age, people usually have no interest in changing. They don't care. They think they've done it all at that point in their lives and don't want anyone telling them what to do.

—But my father is spending a lot of money, and we are very worried. We can't just accept this because the consequences can be even worse.

—Of course, but in my opinion, it's easier for them to try to agree with him on a daily spending limit. Talk to him and offer him, for example, 10 euros a day to spend however he wants. You can open a separate account where they deposit the agreed amount each week and protect the rest of the money with joint accounts. Ideally, you would convince him to come here so we can help him, but I don't think you'll succeed (that was the only thing we both agreed on).

I must admit that at first, I didn't like the idea of opening a separate account for my father to give him money that would only feed his addiction. In fact, I was very surprised that they proposed this measure, and I resisted accepting it as a good solution because, as a former smoker, I had fallen into the trap of trying to quit by reducing the number of cigarettes I smoked daily, and I knew that didn't work. In the best-case scenario, I had managed to hold on for a few days, sometimes not even one because I quickly found an excuse that made me smoke without any control. My theory was that it must be the same with gambling: the access to money had to be cut off completely; I didn't see any intermediate solutions. However, my sisters, who were more moderate in their viewpoints, found it reasonable.

Emotional roller coaster

I spent days and months constantly spinning my thoughts in my head. I would wake up wondering if that day I would go to the bank again to withdraw money, if my parents would make it through the month, or if they would be ruined. That's how it went for a long time. I couldn't concentrate on listening to the radio when I was alone in the car, and I frequently lost track of conversations I had with my family and friends.

Moreover, I would go from feeling like it was all a lie to being monumentally angry at the mess my father had gotten himself into, dragging the family down with him, especially my mother. Other times, I felt sorry for him and even pitied him. I was caught up in a whirlwind of conflicting emotions and exhausted from the relentless search for solutions that always had a catch.

Occasionally, on very specific occasions, especially if something exceptional happened, I would inform my sisters about how my father's addiction was becoming increasingly uncontrollable. They agreed with me that we should talk to him again and, if he didn't listen to reason, we should start taking measures. But the truth is, they weren't willing to take that step. We kept postponing the moment of facing him again and confronting reality.

In the end, despite being terrified of his reaction, I spoke to him again, this time alone. I took advantage of a visit to his house when my mother had gone out shopping. I started by asking him how he felt —without going into details, he said everything was perfect, of course—, and reminded him that I was bringing up the subject again because we were very concerned about his behavior. I mentioned that despite his efforts to control his spending, I had verified that his cash availability was very high, and by the end of the month, their account balances were almost at zero. I said it calmly and affectionately, reiterating that we only wanted to help him and that he needed to admit that he needed help.

—Dad, I'm very uneasy because I see you withdrawing a lot of cash. As you know, much more than what you earn. This situation can't go on for your own good. I know you want to quit, but I'm afraid it's not easy, and you have to accept that.

—I hardly gamble... Just occasionally. Besides, your mother has had a lot of expenses this month because she bought several birthday gifts.

That was false; those gifts represented a minimal portion of their income.

—Dad, you know that my sisters and I are authorized on your accounts, and I've seen that's not the case. By now, I'm certain that you have a real gambling problem. Unfortunately, it's not a harmless hobby you engage in occasionally. You're spending far beyond your means. You've practically depleted your savings, and that cycle needs to stop. Please let us help you. I know you're capable of quitting because you've always shown great willpower, but don't try to solve it on your own because you won't be able to. —He nodded without saying anything—. It's not just for your sake. —I continued as he remained silent, looking at the floor—. Think about Mom too. You don't know what you might need in the future. You're both getting older, and if you ever need to hire some kind of external help, right now you can't afford even a part-time assistant. Let alone a live-in maid or a care facility.

My father kept nodding silently, not looking at me, unsure if he was ashamed or just hoping I would leave him alone.

—Look, since I see you don't have control over the situation, why don't you agree to have joint accounts?

—No! —he responded firmly.

—I thought maybe we could transfer a fixed amount to an account that only you can handle without having to explain anything. With that money, you can do whatever you want, but we'll protect the rest for your well-being.

I admit I didn't like opening up this possibility, but I had to give it a try, accepting the advice from the association I had contacted and the favorable viewpoint of my sisters.

—No. —He said again without hesitation.

—Then what do you think we can do to make this situation less chaotic for everyone?

He didn't respond to that. I think all he wanted was for me to leave him alone and never bring up the subject again. In fact, during this conversation where my father seemed to understand my arguments, I realized that he had no interest in what I was saying. That was the first evidence that he wasn't willing to accept anything that would take away the slightest bit of his freedom to spend money as he pleased. My father didn't want to quit gambling.

He was clever and knew that what I was proposing meant giving up his power. He knew that having a joint signature to withdraw money would require my authorization or that of one of my sisters because if we left that responsibility in my mother's hands, he would likely force her to withdraw money whenever he wanted. That's why he refused and didn't accept any control measures.

While talking to him, I tried to encourage him, insisting that we were on his side and that he wasn't alone in all this. I felt it was important for him to feel comforted and supported by us. I only asked him to understand the consequences of his actions, but without blaming him for anything. I believe that wouldn't have achieved anything, and at the same time, I was certain that it wasn't his fault for falling into the gambling trap because it could happen to anyone. However, I do believe that if a person's actions harm others, they should try to change their behavior. I know asking this of an addict is nearly impossible, but that's my perspective. One can do whatever they want with their own life and possessions without being accountable to anyone, but not with others'.

In summary, we ended the conversation peacefully, but we hadn't made any progress in the direction I intended, in getting my father's commitment—even a minimal one—to rehabilitate himself. It required sacrifices he didn't want to make.

From my side, I deduced that there wasn't much more to talk about with him. He already knew our concern and our willingness to support him. If he changed his mind, he knew he could count on us. If he didn't want to make an effort, our steps would have to focus on protecting what little remained for my mother within the limits allowed by the law, nothing more. Just before leaving his house, I calmly told him that I wouldn't hide the fact that we would continue monitoring the account activities for his and my mother's sake. I explained that I didn't doubt his good intentions, but he needed to understand that in addictions, good intentions often weren't enough. Apparently, only apparently, he understood what I said. Deep down, I knew he didn't like it, and it would put him in a very bad mood, as he eventually demonstrated.

I talked to my sisters —excluding my mother on this occasion— about how fruitless my conversation with him had been. It was evident to all three of us that, given the outcome, sooner or later we would have to take other measures, at least to safeguard the little assets that belonged to my mother.

We knew it wouldn't be easy. In fact, it was the last time I spoke calmly and conciliatorily with my father, and not because I didn't want to. His apparent composure had reached its limit, and his true character would soon emerge.

An Exhausting Search

Despite seeing that my father had no intention of seeking help or admitting his addiction, I persisted in searching for remedies to the irreparable. Thus, in my eagerness to pull my father out of a pit he didn't want to escape from, I devoted too much energy to speaking with experts in gambling addiction.

Although I didn't like what I had to hear right from the start on this new journey through various associations, I reluctantly accepted with great sadness and disappointment that the person who assisted me at the first association was right. They used direct language, perhaps too direct, but accurate. My father was not going to enter any rehabilitation process. In one way or another, every place I went to told me the same thing, but I didn't give up until I spoke with over a dozen of them. I desperately sought a miraculous piece of advice that would shed some light amid all the confusion.

The reality is that none of them could help me because, obviously, it was beyond their control. I encountered kind individuals who, from what I saw, often acted with more goodwill than professionalism. I heard more or less convincing arguments, all of which boiled down to the fact that my father was sick, and we needed to convince him to attend therapy. On one occasion, I spoke with a psychologist who bluntly told me that my father was the owner of his money and could spend it as he pleased. According to him, my father was in full mental capacity and spent his own money—I reminded him that he also spent my mother's if we wanted to be fair—so there was little to be done except to hope he wouldn't have a sudden impulse and spend it all one day. He was right, but I expected to encounter this kind of reasoning in a financial institution, not from an expert in gambling addiction. Perhaps I still struggled to accept such arguments.

So, after several more or less frustrating conversations, I convinced myself that these types of organizations do valuable work but can only help addicts who want to enter a rehabilitation process. If they don't want to take that step, there's nothing that can be done. And even if they do, I sense that the process is very difficult.

Curiously, I found my greatest source of help during this phase in an online forum solely dedicated to gambling addiction. I read many of the threads and came across testimonies of gambling addicts who felt terrible after spending their salaries in an afternoon or accumulating more debt in the hope of recovering lost money. Others admitted to constant lying and the complications they were causing their families due to their addiction.

I also read the opinions of many desperate family members whose father, partner, or child were hooked on gambling, and they didn't know what to do. They had given them many chances, but they kept relapsing and lying. These were heartbreaking stories of families ruined by the same problem.

That's how I discovered the frequently shared advice of one of the moderators, presumably a rehabilitated gambling addict. I decided to register on that forum and privately message them. They responded promptly and offered sensible and very helpful advice. For the first time in many months, I felt like someone understood me. I don't even know their name because they wrote anonymously, but I have a lot to thank them for. The recommendations they gave me are what, in my opinion, should be implemented when dealing with a loved one addicted to gambling.

With a direct but careful style, they told me that the first thing we should do was completely cut off my father's access to money. This also required a commitment from the entire family and friends, who should remain firm when the gambling addict tries to deceive or make excuses to borrow money. If they do provide money, they should know it's at their own risk and they will likely not get it back. They also advised me to explain the situation to other relatives so that they wouldn't lend him money, as gambling addicts are surprisingly resourceful when it comes to lying.

This person accurately predicted how my father would react and insisted that we not allow ourselves to be blackmailed, or we would be lost. They gave me examples of phrases he would use to manipulate us. They were right about everything they said, but we couldn't maintain our firmness. The threats were so severe that we even feared for my mother's safety. Perhaps it was just an emotional power play, but we were afraid to continue down that path. After witnessing my father's irrationality, I expressed this fear to them via email. They said it might not be a simple threat but advised us to assume the risk. Honestly, even at the risk of losing this battle, we couldn't remain steadfast. I believe that you can't always act as dictated by the norms, or sometimes you simply lack the courage to do so.

Theory and Reality

As I have come to acknowledge, my family and I lacked the determination that I now recommend to anyone who has the possibility to exercise it with my father. When my father reacted with great aggression and threats, claiming that it was his money and he could spend it however he wanted, we panicked and felt intimidated.

On the other hand, unless he came to his senses and wanted to cooperate, reality told us that there was little more we could do. I spoke with the directors of the banks where my parents had accounts, and they all agreed that they couldn't prevent him from withdrawing money because he was of sound mind and had authorization to do so.

Once again, they suggested the idea of joint accounts, but we knew that my father would never agree to it. In one of the banks, the person who had been assisting us for years offered to notify us if he requested anything out of the ordinary, such as trying to cancel his savings deposits with my mother. It wasn't an unfounded fear because he had threatened us with doing so as soon as he realized we wanted to impose restrictions on his money. Amid all this madness, he even accused my sisters and me of only wanting his inheritance and claimed he was capable of spending it all and giving it away before leaving us anything. As if he had a fortune. But that's the delusion of a gambling addict.

In short, far from being intimidated, my father grew more defiant. Meanwhile, we were overwhelmed by a growing sense of helplessness because he was spending his money and my mother's, and we couldn't do anything about it. He was entitled to do so because he had full authority over the bank accounts.

They also hinted at the banks and some associations that there was always the option of incapacitating him. I read that in some cases of gambling addiction, incapacity due to prodigality had been approved. If not full incapacity, at least partial, so that it would allow us to protect my mother's assets. I knew this was a lengthy procedure and I was very uncomfortable with the idea, but in my role as an indefatigable investigator, I decided to consult a couple of lawyers. Neither of them seemed convinced that it would be an easy task and they emphasized that he wasn't mentally incapacitated, so there weren't many guarantees of achieving anything.

Furthermore, we were aware that this would create tremendous tension that would make coexistence between my parents impossible. In relation to this, I must say that I often wished my mother would want to divorce because she would have been more at peace, and it would have facilitated many legal matters, but her religious beliefs prevented her from doing so. She resigned herself and believed she had to endure what she had been dealt with.

I set aside the idea of pursuing a legal route, and shortly after, on the recommendation of a friend, I made an appointment with a psychiatrist who was an expert in addictions. When I explained the situation to him, without giving him many details and barely finishing my sentence, he firmly said, "Your father needs to be incapacitated, don't think about it anymore, you have no other solution." He offered to prepare a report to assist us with the procedures, as he insisted that gambling addiction was a mental illness. He explained that he had encountered several cases like this and advised us not to hesitate to do it because my father wouldn't change, and my mother could end up with nothing at a very advanced age. I replied that given the violence with which my father was reacting, I was afraid that something bad would happen to my mother. According to him, this was something inevitable. We had to anticipate it and not give in. Once again, I knew he was right, but everyone knows their circumstances well, and it didn't seem so easy for me to act.

For the time being, it seemed reasonable to protect what belonged to my mother without my father finding out. We spoke to her and explained the situation. She was terrified of taking my father to court due to fear of his reaction, and in a way, I believe she also felt sorry for subjecting him to such a thing. From an outsider's perspective, it's hard to understand feeling compassion for someone who is causing you so much pain, but I didn't feel it was my place to judge my mother's reasons when I, too, sometimes felt sorry for him.

We proposed that she grant us, her daughters, power of attorney, preventing him from selling his house or withdrawing his savings without our consent. Let's say we required her to have co-signing authority, so if my father decided to pressure her into selling her property, mortgaging it, or withdrawing the remaining little money, he would have to obtain our consent. My mother thought this was reasonable, and within a few days, we went to the notary to formalize it. This didn't prevent my father from continuing to spend his and my mother's pension every month —initially, she didn't dare to have her pension deposited into a separate account—, but it meant a lot to us.

Another advantage was that due to his age, my father could no longer request loans, not even from companies that offer easy money in television advertisements. Therefore, when he ran out of money, he would have to deal with it. Fortunately, my sisters and I agreed that if my mother needed anything, we would take care of buying it without him knowing.

Uncontrolled Situation

I became so involved in the problem that I found myself in a dead end. I was aware that the solution was not in my hands, but I couldn't stop trying to find ways to help my parents. I dedicated so much physical and mental time to this that I started to lose enjoyment of my family life, not because I didn't want to be with my husband and children, but because I couldn't handle it anymore. When the weekend came, I lacked the energy to make plans with them, something I had always been proactive about. I also became more irritable, and the worst part was that I didn't know how to regain control of my life.

My husband was always cautious, avoiding expressing opinions on the matter and respecting my decisions, for which I am extremely grateful. Fortunately, my children lived happily unaffected by all of this, and they loved visiting their grandfather, who had always been very affectionate with them. They were also a shield for me when things became more tense because I knew that it was less likely for an argument to arise in front of the children.

Indeed, my relationship with my father worsened, and this was the most difficult part for me. My father, who as I mentioned before always had a bad temper, started showing rude and verbally aggressive reactions a few months after his gambling addiction was discovered, especially towards me. This forced me to assume an extra emotional burden that I was not prepared for and completely threw me off. Unknowingly, my role as a controller and the only one who dared to ask him to acknowledge his problem made me the perfect codependent.

I didn't know what this was, but later I learned that in almost every addiction story, there is the addict and the codependent, who is the family member or close person who monitors them and tries to correct their behavior—usually without success.

I have heard some addicts refer to the codependent as a jailer who makes their life miserable, and I understand perfectly why they perceive it that way. This is what my father must have felt because, behind his usually mild appearance (as his character was very different), he suddenly projected an incredible hatred towards me. It all started one day when I called to see how they were doing, something I did every day. I don't know what triggered his outburst of anger, but he started saying incredibly cruel things out of the blue. I was even more perplexed by his attitude because it had been months since I last talked to him about his addiction.

I didn't like his behavior, but by then, I had accepted that he wouldn't change, and my mother was willing to stand by his side, so I monitored their finances but didn't discuss it with anyone. I thought my mother was more or less protected with the power of attorney, and there wasn't much more we could do unless we started legal proceedings. They were barely making ends meet, struggling to cover fixed expenses, but they managed somehow. My sisters and I had agreed that if circumstances led them to have other needs and assume additional expenses, we would act accordingly.

Going back to the phone conversation on that day, I had to listen to such harsh insults from my father that I started to suspect he was losing his mind, although that wasn't actually the case. I don't want to dwell too much on this matter because it still hurts me deeply to remember certain phrases, but I can assure you that this was the worst part of the whole process.

I witnessed firsthand how my father shamelessly lied, accusing me of stealing money, first to me and then a few days later in front of my mother and sisters. He had created absurd and completely false arguments to convince them that I was the one spending a large portion of his money because I had unrestricted access to his accounts. He also accused me of keeping his credit cards without consulting him, to withdraw money and make payments with them, when the truth is that he, in a burst of goodwill, handed them over to my mother to cancel, and that's exactly what we did.

He was so out of control that I immediately realized it wasn't worth my time to explain to him that everything he was saying was false. Despite his seemingly justified behavior, deep down he knew he was lying, and I wasn't willing to engage in an endless argument where he only wanted to be right at all costs. I was trembling on the other end of the phone because I was hurt by what I was hearing, and I saw that my father had turned into a monster whose cruelty knew no bounds. Despite the pain it caused me, I attributed his reaction to the behavior typical of an addict, as I understood that many reacted with great aggression towards their loved ones.

I was deeply upset and overwhelmed with anxiety, to the point that I had to leave work for a moment to go to a quiet place, call my husband, and try to compose myself because I couldn't stop crying. The most disappointing part was that as the days went by, I realized my father had no intention of apologizing or even showing the slightest hint of remorse.

I discussed this episode with my sisters, and the eldest one said she would talk to him because we couldn't tolerate such excesses. Considering what had happened to me, I thought about the ordeal my mother must have been going through by his side, but she never complained; she only cared about my well-being. In fact, she has never spoken about what it was like to live with my father now that he's no longer here.

My sister went to talk to him two days later. I remember it was a Sunday at noon. She is a composed person and managed to stay calm, but she made it clear that what he had done was outrageous and unfounded. He didn't dare insult her like he did to me, neither at that moment nor in the future, but he showed no signs of remorse whatsoever. On the contrary, according to what she told me when she called later, my father didn't back down during the conversation; he wasn't remorseful. Not only did he maintain and repeat all his accusations and insults against me, but he once again threatened to spend all his money just to leave us with nothing.

Despite my sister's composed approach, he confronted her and demanded respect for all of us. It was futile trying to make him understand that we only wanted his well-being and that his behavior would lead him nowhere. He didn't care at all; he threatened to do terrible things and even had the audacity to suggest to my sister that she should talk to me and demand that I stop looking at his accounts. If I agreed, he would forget about all the harm he was causing and make peace with me. That's how clear and straightforward he was.

From that moment on, my relationship with my father had a before and an after. I decided, among other things, that I wouldn't give in to his blackmail, that I wouldn't give up seeing my mother, and that we wouldn't be separated from the rest of the family. I also decided to maintain emotional distance and not argue with him. This helped me a lot because more episodes like the one described would come later. The difference was that by then, I had learned to approach it differently, without letting myself be manipulated.

Indeed, regardless of my attitude, he sought conflict with me from time to time. Luckily, during that phase, I was already attending therapy, and my psychologist helped me understand many things that I will explain later. She said that my father was reproducing the cycles of an abuser with me. First, they accumulate tension, often without valid reasons—she emphasized this a lot because I often felt guilty for triggering those outbursts of aggression—then they explode, and then comes the so-called honeymoon phase. This is the phase where they soften, try to get closer, and seek reconciliation. My therapist also believed that my father— who never asked for forgiveness but did try to give me a gift a couple of times, which I politely declined—wasn't seeking my forgiveness out of remorse but because he was aware that he had gone too far and needed to normalize things.

I found it impossible to believe that my father could go that far. I didn't recognize the father he had been during my childhood and adolescence. As I always tried to justify it, I assured my psychologist that he was behaving that way because gambling had driven him crazy, but she told me that perhaps my father was always like that and that his addiction brought out the worst in him.

However, I think it's important to emphasize that not all gambling addicts behave like this. In fact, in my conversations with some of them, I have detected a sense of guilt that my father never expressed, although he might have felt it. Every person is different, and generalizations cannot be made. I can only recount what I have experienced.

The side effects

My father's aggression towards me seriously affected my family and professional life. Until then, I had periods of anxiety that alternated with a few calmer days, even though they were few and far between. But then I entered a cycle of constant anxiety from which I didn't know how to escape. I could hardly sleep, I had constant heart palpitations, and I struggled to perform well at work. My profession requires a lot of attention, and I feared making mistakes that could cost me my job. Fortunately, that didn't happen because I decided to seek treatment as soon as possible, and fortunately, the activity in my industry was slower at that time, and the workdays were more manageable.

In any case, living a normal life, even if only for a few hours, while isolating myself from the problem, was almost impossible for me. Thoughts bombarded me with my father's words, as if they were engraved in my mind and couldn't be erased. I always had a fear that something bad would happen, even if it had nothing to do with my father's addiction. I was diagnosed with generalized anxiety disorder, from which I have fully recovered today.

I understood that for my own well-being and that of my family, I couldn't continue like that. So I stopped searching for ways to help my father and focused on helping myself. I had forgotten that I should prioritize myself and learn to take care of myself above all else.

Change of priorities

At first, I found a psychologist who was making an effort to reduce my anxiety levels, but my progress was limited, and I was still struggling despite my efforts. I honestly explained how I felt and decided to suspend therapy. I mention this because I believe it's crucial to have a good connection with your psychologist, and sometimes it's not achieved on the first try.

A few weeks later, I read an article online that was closely related to my situation and was written by the psychologist I had been seeing for years. I immediately got in touch with her, and with her help, I was fortunate enough to understand many things and change some ideas that were proving very detrimental to me in my circumstances. Gradually, I was able to sort out the chaos within me and address my codependency, or at least become fully aware of it.

Since my level of anxiety was overwhelming, she recommended that I see a doctor to prescribe medication that would help me sleep and be somewhat calmer. Initially, they suggested taking anti-anxiety medication only when I was very nervous to see how I responded. If that wasn't enough, they would consider a stronger and longer-term treatment.

Thanks to psychological therapy and the relaxation sessions we also incorporated, I was able to gradually reduce my constant nervousness with patience and consistency and limit the medication to taking an anti-anxiety drug only when I couldn't handle it anymore. It was the first time I had been prescribed this type of medication, and I admit I had some reservations about getting hooked on them and not being able to stop. I shared this fear with the doctor, and they reassured me by explaining that it was fine to take them only in very specific moments or for a period. That's what I did, and I never experienced withdrawal symptoms when I stopped taking them.

I want to clarify at this point that if I had needed a stronger treatment, I would have requested it. I also recommend to people who need it not to resist seeking help if they find themselves unable to control the situation. Sometimes, the body becomes so imbalanced that it can't return to normal without chemical assistance.

When I started psychological therapy, I had already accepted that my father was not going to stop gambling, and our relationship was unlikely to normalize. For my own physical and mental health, I decided that I would never again ask him to stop wasting money on slot machines. After offering him unconditional support so many times before, I trusted that if he ever wanted to climb out of the hole he had gotten himself into, he knew we were there for whatever he needed. In the meantime, I wanted my life to continue as normally as possible, regardless of his decisions.

It wasn't easy, by any means, as he continued to be aggressive towards me from time to time. There was another very tough moment when he tried to withdraw his savings and realized that my mother also needed one of us to consent. We had arranged with the bank that, upon maturity, that money would be in my mother's name, anticipating that he might try to take it, just as he had done with the rest of the savings. This once again infuriated him, but we were accustomed to his fits of rage, and this time he understood that he couldn't always do as he pleased. He had no choice but to endure it, although his bad mood was almost constant. His animosity towards me became even more evident during incidents like this, but I had come to terms with it.

I was also struck by his constant ability to lie. For example, he always played the victim card and believed that his excesses were justified by the aftermath of his illness, but it baffled me when one day he would tell me he was feeling terrible and could barely walk, yet I knew he had been to the bank and then to the bars. He would also boast during some family gatherings and claim to have a lot of money. All of this angered me, and I had to make a great effort not to voice my thoughts because it would only lead to another confrontation.

Fortunately, I grew stronger and less vulnerable to his manipulations. When he had fits of anger, I couldn't find it in myself to argue with him or even try to reason with him. I'm not inclined towards confrontation by nature, but at that time, I avoided it more than ever. However, I did learn to be assertive and not back down in the face of his attacks. When this happened, I would respond seemingly calm (though I was very nervous inside) and firmly, showing him that I wasn't afraid.

On one occasion, he told me that he had started gambling again —as if he had ever stopped— just to spite us because, according to him, we were neglecting him despite his good behavior. I told him that he was free to do whatever he wanted and that, although in my opinion, he had chosen the wrong path, I respected his choice. I also reminded him that he couldn't count on me to support him in continuing down that path, but I would be there for him if he ever decided to get out of it.

I handled my relationship with my father differently, but due to my nature, every time I experienced one of these episodes, I would become unsettled and suffer. However, luckily, it took me less and less time to regain normalcy in my life.

I was becoming aware of how important my well-being was, something that seemed to have been forgotten. However, except for rare exceptions, humans are not masochistic and eventually flee from what causes them suffering. In this sense, I was no different, so to avoid being systematically targeted by my father's anger, I had to distance myself physically and emotionally from him.

It was very complicated, although I have the ability to control my emotions well, so it wasn't apparent how much I struggled each time I visited his house. I still remember the stomachaches I would get every time I went there because I didn't know what to expect. I spoke to my mother every day, but I saw them much less, and when I did, it was for a shorter time. I tried not to go to his house alone almost ever, and we never stayed overnight - always with some excuse about my children or husband's obligations - and I tried to coordinate with one of my sisters to be there. We had noticed that this way, he was less likely to confront us.

I also noticed that he was always tremendously kind to my husband and children. My husband always responded politely, despite being more aware than anyone of how my father treated me. My children, oblivious to everything, were always delighted when we took them.

However, I couldn't wait to leave. I never managed to overcome this feeling; I just dealt with it as best as I could. Sometimes, I felt like telling my mother to meet outside of their house so we could spend some time together, but I didn't want to put her in that position. Above all, I tried to avoid tensions, for myself and my family, so brief meetings seemed to work. I still maintained a courteous relationship with my father, but I was no longer capable of showing him affection.

In therapy, I had to work extensively on the guilt that would surface every time I left my parents' house, but I gradually managed to overcome it. My therapist played a decisive role in helping me accept that I was mistaken in a preconceived notion that most people have - that your parents, by virtue of being your parents, are always good and love you.

As I mentioned before, I often used to say that my father had become that way because of the gambling, that he was sick, but she argued that it wasn't entirely true, that my father already had a certain personality, and if anything, his addiction was revealing his cruel side. Perhaps that was true, but I still don't understand why my father acted that way. I remember one occasion when I was at his house - I had gone alone exceptionally - and witnessed him starting to unleash one of his episodes on my mother. I immediately confronted him, telling him that enough was enough. Very angrily, he told me that he was going to die soon and repeated all those phrases and judgments he had been saying for over thirty years to portray himself as the victim.

I tried to have a moment alone with him and tell him that he was mistaken in his attitude and that it deeply saddened me to see him harming himself. He yelled at me that he didn't want to hear me, told me to shut up, and said I didn't need to come to his house. If it were up to him, I would have stopped seeing him years ago. It was ten years with this situation, and there were many moments when I never wanted to see him again, but if the price was not seeing my mother, I wasn't willing to accept it. On the other hand, I believe that with his provocations, he was trying to drive us apart from her, something we were not going to allow.

With my sisters, he was always more moderate, so it wasn't as difficult for them to go see them. I gradually stopped taking care of various household matters that I used to manage, and they took over in my place. In the last year, I think it was also very difficult for them because my father was unbearable. He was angry all the time and complained about everything. I could see that, in his final stage, my mother and my sisters were also unable to show him affection. His irritable nature made everyone around him avoid him.

He probably realized that we were affectionate with my mother and among ourselves. I imagine that he saw himself becoming increasingly lonely, but that was what he had chosen. I always held onto the hope that one day he would hit rock bottom - they say that's what addicts need to change - and recognize his addiction, but he didn't. I understand that he may have had his reasons, but in my opinion, his obstinacy came at a very high emotional cost for him.

All these experiences also taught me not to judge the decisions that other people make regarding their loved ones. I have always tried not to judge anyone, but now it doesn't even cross my mind to make the slightest evaluation. Not all families are perfect, and I believe in maintaining unity among everyone, but there are situations that are unsustainable.

When I hear criticism about children who don't visit their parents or parents who distance themselves from their children, before continuing to listen, I try to cut the conversation off by saying that we need to understand all perspectives. I remain very vocal about this because certain comments can cause a lot of harm.

Even I, who was educated in a religious school and consider myself a believer, used to think years ago that parents always act in the best interest of their children and that as children, we should be grateful to them. However, life has disproven this theory, and there's no need to make a big deal out of it. Sometimes I watch those TV shows where people seek forgiveness and reconciliation with their families after many years of distance due to addiction or other circumstances. Before my experience, it saddened me when the family wanted nothing to do with that person, but now I understand very well why they decide to keep their distance. For them, it's simply a way to protect themselves.

As I write this, I think about those who find it difficult to stop seeing their gambling-addicted family member - or someone with another addiction - even though it's ruining their lives. I put myself in the shoes of their partners and the children who live in the same household. I know it's very difficult to take that step. It took me a lot to distance myself partially. I made the decision when I saw that my father not only didn't want to quit his addiction but also became increasingly aggressive; that was the real trigger.

I believe that this is the best way out when the addict is destroying themselves and others, when peaceful coexistence and a dignified life for everyone are no longer possible. I don't think anyone has the right to cause this harm to their environment. I emphasize that the addict is not to blame for falling into their illness, but they are responsible for getting out of it.

In any case, everyone knows their circumstances and knows how they should act. I've already mentioned that I wished my mother would leave my father, but she lived with him until the end because she believed it was what she should do, and we had to respect her wishes.

Another perspective

During the years I attended psychotherapy, I experienced great progress, but from time to time, especially in the beginning, I felt like I was stuck and even regressing. It was simply part of the process.

In the first year, I had a weekly session. Then it became biweekly, every three weeks, and in the last years, I went once a month, but I never stopped seeing the psychologist.

After a long time, I realized that if my father was a gambling addict, I perfectly embodied the figure of the emotional codependent, a term I had never heard until it was applied to me. In reality, I discovered this attachment, and then my therapist gave it a name.

To explain it simply: codependent people have an excessive concern for other people's problems to the point that we make them our own and want to solve them, without knowing where the limit is or how far we should go. We abandon our own lives to pretend to solve others'.

Codependents are unaware of the basic rules of any rescue manual. An example that helped me understand how we think is one of the instructions given to us when we fly: in case we must put on the oxygen mask due to an emergency, we must first put it on ourselves and then help our children and others who may need assistance. If we don't act this way, we may lose consciousness, and not only would we endanger our own lives, but also those of others whom we wouldn't be able to help anymore.

Well, something seemingly easy to understand is very complex for the codependent. They will think it's selfish to save themselves first and then take care of others.

One of the first instructions my psychologist gave me was to stop monitoring my parents' accounts on a daily basis. Since stopping to watch their account movements was a world to me, I agreed with her to do it only every two weeks. She thought it was good, and so I did. I always kept this agreement, and it greatly relieved me from the daily emotional burden I had taken upon myself without anyone asking me to.

I came to understand that my father's visits to the bank or the bars were not going to change whether I checked his accounts more often or not. What my father did, whether I liked it or not, depended solely on him, and I had to respect that. After a while, I reduced this monitoring to once a month, and I maintained that rhythm for over a year. My psychologist didn't pressure me to space it out more; I suppose she was aware that I had to take the initiative if I wanted to torture myself less with my periodic checks. For my part, I had a strict discipline not to violate the "once a month" rule, nothing more. I convinced myself that my father spent as he pleased whatever income he had each month. They covered his basic expenses, and then they ended the month in a tight situation, but that was how it was.

Suddenly, one day I woke up particularly lucid and decided that I was going to lift that self-imposed penance of monitoring the accounts. I don't know why, but I told myself that not one more day. I thought I had been enduring that tension for too long and naively waiting for a miracle to solve the problem. I saw very clearly that I had to be the one to find the solution, without waiting for my father to do anything. And so I did. That day I «granted myself the freedom» and felt a great relief. If there were any problems, I would find out about them. When I mentioned it to my psychologist, she thought it was a magnificent decision and congratulated me for it.

Some time later, I received a call from the bank because my parents' account was overdrawn, and they couldn't pay the community fee. I immediately covered the payment but told my sisters that our mother's pension would come out of that checking account. We agreed on it, and we presented it to our mother without giving her the option to choose. Since she was excessively worried about appearing as a defaulter in her community, she didn't oppose it, and my younger sister took care of telling it to my father. He defended himself by saying that the person from the bank was exaggerating, but the decision had been made, and there was no turning back. My sister told him that since he couldn't control the situation and wanted to continue playing freely, we had to protect at least my mother's money. When her account reached zero, there would be no more slot machines that month.

This step was a relief from an economic standpoint because, from an emotional perspective, the tension was growing increasingly higher. My mother's pension was lower, and this alone didn't solve the problem because if the circumstances required us to hire external help to take care of them, my father's pension would be necessary. For now, with my mother having a separate account with her pension, we knew that fixed expenses were covered and they wouldn't lack the essentials. We agreed that she wouldn't have cash at home. We would do the shopping online, and all payments would be made through the bank. She left a certain amount of cash at one of my sister's houses and would go there when she needed to make small payments with cash.

It wasn't fair, nor was it very instructive, to allow my father to use his pension solely for his addiction while my mother, earning much less, supported the entire family's finances. But it also wasn't fair for him to spend my mother's pension and accumulate debts. It was the lesser of two evils, considering that he had full control over his money.

He never cared about how the food and other expenses were paid. He lived his life, coming and going as he pleased, and seemingly, nothing bothered him. My mother knew the bars he went to gamble at. I assume that since she found out about his addiction, she came across him more than once, but it didn't make a difference. She told us that on one occasion, she stood in front of the bar's window while he mindlessly played. According to her, he glanced at her, continued playing, and left without saying anything, neither at that moment nor when he arrived home.

Another time, my mother entered a café with some friends and found him there gambling. Apparently, that day he won a considerable amount of money. He kept it to himself and left without greeting them. My mother was so afraid of him that she didn't dare confront him when they met at home that night. Now I think she did the right thing because any confrontation with him was counterproductive.

These are just a few examples of how gambling completely absorbs people to the point that they can't see beyond their bets. My father had only one passion, slot machines, and everything else was indifferent to him. I don't doubt that he felt bad in many moments, but gambling was his sole priority, and it dominated him until the end. I still remember how, almost dragging his leg because he walked with great difficulty, we would finish eating, and without saying anything, he would put on his coat and say he was going for a walk, even in the middle of winter with tremendous cold. We live in a very cold city, but for him, there was no snow, wind, or anything that would deter him from going to the bar.

On the contrary, he refused to go to the pharmacy or other nearby establishments because he felt unwell. My mother always took care of those errands. It was unfair, but I believe that he saw it as the most normal thing. His perspective was that of an addict, unable to see beyond a slot machine. Especially in the last years, he didn't make an effort to disguise his selfishness or lack of empathy towards others. There were several instances where he demonstrated that he didn't care about what happened to us, but that was his illness.

The End of the Story

My father died at the age of 88, and he kept gambling as long as he could walk and go to the bank to withdraw money to play. He continued doing so until two weeks before his passing.

One summer day, he fell in the street and couldn't walk again. We had to hospitalize him, and he never returned home. We were all with him until the end, especially my mother, my sisters, and myself, although it wasn't easy. His character became even more violent in his final days. He was disrespectful towards us and the healthcare staff. One day, we had to call the psychiatrist to see if they could calm him down. Before being alone with my father, I explained that he might be experiencing withdrawal symptoms due to his addiction. After talking to him, the doctor told me that there wasn't much they could do because my father didn't acknowledge his gambling addiction, nothing new. They prescribed him medication to calm him down, but at times, he would become aggressive again. I hinted to the psychiatrist that, considering my father's old age, he might not be mentally sound, and I was surprised by his response:

«Your father is perfectly sane, perhaps too much so from what I've observed. Your father has a bad temper, don't overthink it».

I thanked him for his honesty, and he told me not to excuse his behavior just because he was older.

Despite everything, my father was not alone during those days. We made sure he was always accompanied. He also received many visits from other relatives and friends. However, I believe he died very lonely, with the same solitude he had sought in recent years. He didn't allow us to get close to him emotionally, rather the opposite.

Although it may seem naive on my part, I always held onto the hope that my father would have a kind or reconciliatory gesture before leaving. I had heard that many people try to make peace with their loved ones before departing. In my father's case, it didn't happen, and it left me with great sadness, but I also understand that, for whatever reason, he chose it that way.

As for me, I believe I did what I had to do. I spent many hours alone with him in the hospital because I had taken time off, and my husband and children were away. My mother, my sisters, and I did our best to make him comfortable and tried to cheer him up, even though he didn't appreciate it.

My father passed away on the exact day I had left on a trip to spend the holidays with my family. He seemed to be doing better, and one of my sisters had more availability and stayed with him. As soon as I arrived at my destination, she called me to say that he had worsened and had only a few hours left to live. We immediately returned, but he had already passed away when we arrived. Just in case, I had silently said my goodbyes to him on the last day I was at the hospital. Despite the doctors saying he was improving; I had a feeling that it was the last time I would see him.

I won't hide the fact that when my father left, I also felt a sense of relief because it marked the end of a ten-year period that felt eternal and was filled with great pain, despite managing my emotions better. Breaking a family bond hurts a lot, even as an adult. I would say it's even worse when you're older because you're much more aware of everything. They say that children have a greater capacity to better assimilate that pain, I don't know.

At the same time, I experienced a different kind of mourning than usual because I had already mourned while my father was alive. I had emotionally said goodbye to him years ago to be able to move forward with my life. I think something similar happened to my mother and sisters.

After focusing more on myself and my family, there were moments when I was very happy. I experienced significant personal events with my husband and children, and I successfully undertook professional projects that were very rewarding. It's not that I stopped caring about my father's addiction and its consequences, but I only did so when necessary. I no longer insisted on solving the impossible or fixing what was beyond my control. If my father had wanted to change, I would have gladly supported him, but things don't always happen as we wish. Nonetheless, life goes on, and we must find happiness. That depends on us, on no one else.

An Addiction, Two Perspectives

Although this book is written with the families and loved ones of gamblers in mind, I wanted to understand how this disease is experienced from both sides. I believe that the expressed feelings are very similar to those of other addictions, but here I focus on gambling, which is the one I know best.

To undertake this project, I reached out to a rehabilitation center and requested permission to speak with some gamblers. My aim was to try to understand their behavior. Deep down, I sought to better comprehend my father and find answers to the many mysteries he left behind. I am grateful to all those who generously shared their testimonies with me.

I also attended a support group for families of gambling addicts. I found great solace in listening to their stories. I extend my gratitude to all of them for dedicating their time and sharing their insights with me.

In the Shoes of a Compulsive Gambler

I met Juanma, a 43-year-old bus driver, divorced with two children. At that moment, he was particularly devastated because he had relapsed after nearly a year of not playing slot machines.

—I feel terrible. Like many other times, I had made a promise to myself not to gamble, and everything was going well. I had gone almost ten months without spending a single coin, but once again, I fell back into it. In just one week, I've blown my entire month's salary. I don't even know how I'm going to get through the rest of the month. My ex-wife keeps calling me because I haven't paid child support, and she fears the worst. As always, I lie and keep stalling. I feel like complete garbage.

—Could you explain what happened? Was there a reason that led to your relapse?

—I always find excuses, but after more than 20 years in this hole, I know they're worthless. I can't keep deceiving myself. This disease is so treacherous. You think you've overcome it, and one day, for no apparent reason, you tempt fate, and you're caught up in it again. I could tell you that something terrible happened that drove me to gamble again, but this time, I don't even have the desire to justify myself.

—Have you quit before?

—Yes, six times, but I never lasted as long as this last time. Within two or three months at most, I was back to gambling. It's despairing because you try and try again, but I always end up falling back into it.

—At least you're trying to quit. Others in your situation don't even acknowledge they have an addiction.

—Yeah... but I'm exhausted. I'm starting to think that I'll never make it, that I'm not capable of doing it, and that's what frustrates me. I think maybe I have to resign myself to being trapped in this mess, accepting that I'll never be able to live a normal life.

—Who do you live with, Juanma?

—With my parents, since I got divorced two years ago. My ex-wife got tired, rightfully so, of putting up with me. She was fed up with believing my lies, giving me chance after chance for nothing. We never made it through the month without difficulties. The hardest part was when we had to take our children out of extracurricular activities because we couldn't afford them. I think that was the last straw. When she told me she was leaving, I got furious and said all sorts of things, but I have no right to blame her, quite the opposite. My children and she deserve a better life.

—How do your parents deal with your addiction?

—Well, they do what they can. They're already old, and they have enough on their plate taking care of themselves. We barely talk about the subject. They provide me a place to live, but they haven't given me money for years. Neither have any other family members. I've caused them enough trouble as it is.

— Besides money, what else have you lost because of gambling?

—Everything, except my job, which I've luckily managed to hold onto. But I've lost my ex-wife, my brothers hardly talk to me, and I've disappointed my children. That's what hurts the most. Plus, when I'm not gambling, I see that my life is so much better, but the gambling takes hold of me.

—In those moments, don't you think about the harm you're causing yourself and your loved ones?

—Honestly, no. At least, I think about it afterwards when I've lost everything, and I realize what I've done. But while I'm gambling, it's as if I lose all sense of reason. I can't think or focus on anything other than the game. I delude myself into thinking I'll win a fortune and use it to pay off my debts, and then reality hits me hard.

Mario is 28 years old and has been gambling-free for 13 months. He was hooked on online gambling for 6 years until one day his parents caught him and understood where his money was going.

—I worked as a call center operator, and I had a pretty average, if not low, salary. Sometimes I earned extras with certain campaigns, but it was not much. Until just over a year ago, my obsession was coming home and blowing all the money I earned, and even what I didn't earn, on online bets. I started off playing around, just to see what would happen, and the worst thing that could've happened is that I got lucky and won a few tens of euros. That was my downfall. I got hooked and never won again, but I couldn't stop trying my luck, hoping to replicate that first day.

—Did you gamble only when you were at home?

—Generally, yes. As soon as I got home, I would go to my room with my computer and forget about the time. Fortunately for me, we couldn't use mobile phones at work, but lately, I took advantage of breaks to go to the restroom and gamble. I commuted to work on a motorcycle, which saved me some money.

—Didn't your parents realize you were spending a lot of money?

—It took them years, and thankfully they caught me. They should've been more suspicious of the lies I told them. They have a successful business, so they didn't have financial problems. They spend a lot of time away from home, and sometimes they're traveling, so I was left to my own devices at home. My brother went abroad to work, so no one was keeping an eye on me.

—How did you have so much money available?

—Well, I dropped out of school at 18, and my parents forced me to fend for myself. They said I needed to learn the value of hard-earned money. I was always diligent with work, never faltered in that regard, but my salary didn't provide much, so I started making up stories about additional studies I wanted to pursue: languages, web page programming... My parents thought I was getting serious about the importance of being prepared, imagine that. I convinced them to open a credit card for me through the company to cover all these expenses, and I used it solely for gambling. I knew that only the people in the finance department would review the transactions, and they wouldn't expose me. But one day, my mother, who already suspected I wasn't really studying much, requested the statement for my card, and that's when everything came to light.

—How much did you spend?

—A lot. At least 4,000 a month. Some months, it reached 6,000 or more.

—Once you were caught, did you decide to quit?

—Well, they forced me to quit by cutting off all my sources of funding. My parents talked to me and said that the game was over, and I had to abide by the rules. They canceled the internet at home, gave me a phone without data, and made me work in their company's warehouse without a computer, under constant surveillance. In reality, I don't even have access to my own salary. It all goes into a savings account. If I go out with friends, they know they can't lend me money, and I only go out with just enough for a drink. I also attend this rehabilitation group every week.

—Does this situation of control overwhelm you?

—I won't lie to you... It hit me hard when they took everything away from me all at once, but I know it's the best thing that could have happened. Today, I'm grateful because I don't know how far I would have gone with my madness. Now, I even feel fortunate because my parents uncovered the truth, and from the very beginning, they've been very strict with the rules.

—Do you still have the urge to gamble?

—Sometimes, yes, but I know what that entails. Now, I also don't have the opportunity to gamble because someone always accompanies me. Thanks to this constant vigilance, I haven't relapsed, but it will take time for me to forget about gambling. Here, I've met other people in my situation, and we're well aware that we can never let our guard down.

—What are you most afraid of?

—I think flying alone. I don't know how I'll react when I'm no longer monitored around the clock. I still don't have that much confidence in myself. I would also like to have a girlfriend, but I'm afraid that no one would want me with this addiction.

—What do they tell you here when you express these fears?

—They say it's all a matter of time and that I'm in a process of rehabilitation. Everything will come in due course. For me, going 13 months without gambling is already a great achievement. I have a family that fully supports me, and I consider myself very fortunate.

In the Shoes of a Family Member

Manuela is a nurse, 38 years old, and has been married to a gambling addict for 12 years. They have two daughters, aged 9 and 6.

—Today is one of those days when I can't take it anymore. I'm desperate, this is not living for me, nor for my daughters. I've cornered my husband countless times, and his intentions to quit gambling only last for two days. Then he always goes back to the same habits. I've always carried the weight of the family finances. He has never taken responsibility for anything. I wish my daughters could participate in more activities, but we can't afford it because their father doesn't contribute a single euro. I have a reasonable salary, but it's not enough. And it's not just about him spending his salary on this nonsense; he's becoming more unbearable every day. When he loses or has nothing left, my daughters and I have to endure his fits of rage and disrespect. I've considered leaving him several times, but I think this time it's definitive.

—What keeps you by his side?

—Despite everything, I feel sorry for him. I think I stopped being in love with him years ago, but I lack the strength to end all of this. I always end up believing his lies and making excuses for him because this is an illness. He's not to blame for being addicted to gambling.

—What does your family think about all of this?

—I barely talk to them. It hurts them to see what I'm going through, and they disagree with me staying with my husband. My mother has told me many times that if he wants to ruin his life, he can do it, but he shouldn't waste my life or our daughters' lives. However, it angers me so much when they say that, and in the end, I find myself more and more alone.

—Are your daughters aware of what's happening to their father?

—Not exactly. They witness many arguments between us, and the atmosphere at home is not good, but they don't know the true cause. I feel guilty for not having the courage to start over alone with them; I think I'm causing them a lot of harm.

—Why do you attend a support group for family members of gambling addicts?

—Because here I can express how I feel without being judged, and because I know I need help to confront my husband and, if he doesn't quit gambling, to leave him.

—What do the people who attend here tell you?

— They tell me that I have to think about myself and not try to solve my husband's messes without demanding anything from him. He is selfish and doesn't think about us. I know I can't continue like this; I've cried too much already because of all this.

Azucena is 42 years old and has a 7-year-old son. She works as a shop assistant in a department store. She has suffered a lot due to her husband's addiction to slot machines, but she feels much better since she started working on her codependent behavior. In her case, the change in attitude led her husband to attempt rehabilitation.

—I spent nine years chasing after my husband, going into bars to take him home, talking to the bar owners where he played to prevent them from giving him change or allowing him to play. I cried and suffered day after day, and he didn't make the slightest effort to quit. I felt overwhelmed and couldn't see a way to fix my life until one day, I don't know why yet, I decided to stand up for myself. I got very serious and told him that enough was enough. Either he stopped playing with all the controls that entailed, or he wouldn't enter the house that night. He thought I was bluffing, but I did it. He had to go to his parents' house for a while. I told him that he had already made our lives miserable enough and that, as long as he played, he couldn't count on me.

—Did you start taking better care of yourself?

—Absolutely, from day one. Gradually, I started reclaiming my social life, exercising, and enjoying things that had disappeared from my life years ago. It felt like a luxury to prepare a meal and sit at the table with my son without being on edge, fearing when his father would arrive and in what state. Peace returned to our lives, and I wouldn't trade that for anything. I've suffered and cried enough for him.

—Do you know how he's doing now?

—Well, surprisingly, he has been gambling-free for six months. Look, after so many years of monitoring him, he took the step without anyone demanding it. He still lives with his parents and regularly sees my son. For the first time in these months, he contributed money for our son's expenses. I know he's making a great effort. He lives with his parents and keeps track of all his expenses for them, even for a cup of coffee, as they tell me. I'm surprised, and I'm really happy for him.

—How is your relationship at the moment?

—We get along really well, like never before. We talk calmly about things. Honestly, I don't recognize him; he's a completely different person.

—Would you get back together with him?

—Yes, because I still love him, but I want to wait for some time. He knows and understands that. Right now, our priority is his recovery and enjoying this moment, which is an immense gift for us.

Lessons Learned

We learn from everything, although there are times when we wish we hadn't gone through certain lessons. These are the lessons that my experience with my father taught me.

— Addictions don't discriminate based on age, gender, social status, or economic condition. We are all susceptible to addiction.

— We should not judge anyone for being trapped by an addiction or for not being able to quit.

— The addict is a sick person.

— We can only help our addicted loved ones when they accept that they have a problem and ask for help.

— The addict may have fallen into the game without realizing it, but only they can decide whether to abandon their addiction.

— Sometimes, even if it hurts or we don't like it, we have to let our loved ones make mistakes.

— When the addict and the consequences of their addiction interfere with and harm family life, the healthiest thing to do is to create distance.

— We are not obligated to endure everything just because the addict is our family member.

— The only way to protect oneself when the addict does not recognize their disease or allow themselves to be helped is to let them go their own way.

— The addict must know that, as long as they don't change, they won't have our complicity in fueling their addiction. Likewise, they should know that if they truly want to overcome their addiction, we will be there to support them.

Reflections of a Rehabilitated Gambling Addict

For gambling addicts:

— Gambling makes you lose money and your entire life. For years, I wanted to start various businesses, but it all went down the drain because of gambling. Now I know what it's like to have a fulfilling life.

— It's not enough to abstain from gambling for a while. I had to convince myself that gambling couldn't have the slightest space in my life. Not even for a small bet in the lottery. NOTHING.

— Don't set long-term goals. Make a commitment to quit gambling for the next 24 hours and renew it day by day.

— The journey is difficult, you will struggle, but gradually you will start feeling happier.

— You can overcome this, I speak from experience, but it requires willpower and complete conviction. There is another life without gambling that is worth living.

— We never stop being sick, so don't let your guard down, even if you have been rehabilitated for years.

For the family members of a gambling addict:

— The worst part of this addiction is not the money we lose but the emotions we lose. There comes a point where the only thing that motivates us is gambling, and we don't care about anything else happening around us. We lose our families, but it doesn't matter to us; we have lost the ability to feel.

— The only way to regain our true selves is by overcoming our addiction, but this will happen when we decide, not when our loved ones tell us to.

— We are liars, manipulators, and blackmailers.

— If you are codependent, take care of yourself. We will never tire of directing our anger towards you.

— When we truly decide to quit, we will need our family's support more than ever.

— There is no explanation for our behavior, don't try to find one because we don't even have it.

— Don't give us access to money or give in to our blackmail out of fear of the consequences.

— If we agree to undergo rehabilitation, it must come with control measures. You must be strict with them and demand that we justify every penny to you.

José Manuel, 58 five years (five years without gambling)

Is responsible gambling possible?

Gambling is more accessible than ever today. The internet is filled with online betting sites, gambling establishments are growing in large cities, and television bombards us with advertisements featuring popular athletes and other figures encouraging people to gamble, especially during sports broadcasts.

At the same time, news reports highlight the alarming increase of gambling addiction among young people, mainly due to online gambling. I can only imagine the suffering experienced by those addicts and their families.

We are faced with a legal activity, but I can't help but wonder why authorities don't prohibit advertising that encourages gambling. I know that some television networks have already decided to ban this type of advertising, and I hope that, similar to what was done with alcohol and tobacco in the past, it will eventually disappear from all advertising platforms.

Many may argue that those who are addicted haven't quit because they no longer see advertisements, and they may be right. However, I see no reason to promote any behavior that can become addictive. Perhaps there are significant economic interests that not only prevent the cessation of advertising but also create more barriers to accessing gambling.

On the other hand, it's reasonable to assume that those who gamble are adults and should know their limits, where the boundary lies. I agree with this notion, but I'm not sure where that line is drawn. I suspect that one realizes too late that they have fallen into a hole from which it is very difficult to escape.

Don't miss out!

Visit the website below and you can sign up to receive emails whenever Patricia de León publishes a new book. There's no charge and no obligation.

https://books2read.com/r/B-A-JTHEB-EMIYC

BOOKS 2 READ

Connecting independent readers to independent writers.

About the Author

I am a journalist with training in coaching, social media, and corporate communication. Patricia de León is the pseudonym I use to share my experiences and the conclusions of some research work I have conducted. In this case, I speak about a firsthand experience, and out of respect for all the individuals I mention, especially my father, I keep my identity and theirs anonymous. My intention is to inspire other people who may be going through the same situation. Whether they know my real name or not won't make a difference in helping them.

My professional experience has mainly been in the field of communication and written journalism. Additionally, I am studying personal coaching because I believe it is a very useful way to achieve goals.

Thank you for reaching this point. If you have any suggestions or inquiries, you can contact me at:

yoaestonojuego@gmail.com